Lace & Pyrite

Letters from Two Gardens

Ross Gay & Aimee Nezhukumatathil

Copyright © 2014 by Aimee Nezhukumatathil & Ross Gay

Originally published by Organic Weapon Arts

All rights reserved. No part of this book may be reproduced in any manner without written consent except for the quotation of short passages used inside of an article, criticism, or review.

Get Fresh Books Publishing, A NonProfit Corp.

PO BOX 901

Union, New Jersey 07083

www.gfbpublishing.org

ISBN: 978-1-7345802-7-3

Library of Congress Control Number: 2021933599

Cover design & book layout: Sara Pinsonault

Author photo by Soleil Davíd

Contents

Introduction

SUMMER
AUTUMN
WINTER
SPRING
SUMMER

Our Wholeness, Our Togetherness…
Acknowledgements

An Introduction

In the late July swelter and dragonfly buzz of the summer of 2011, we began a poem correspondence, based on no prompts, no assignments—just that we were to send a poem at least once a week, maybe more if we were lucky. We were just going to hold each other accountable knowing someone was waiting for our poem three states away. Happy mail. Turns out he's one of my few friends who still loves the tactile pleasure of writing letters—an easy enough project I thought would surely end by the time I visited him in his hometown of Bloomington, Indiana that September.

But something happened during that visit that made us change our minds. We toured the Bloomington Community Orchard, and he showed me around his own organic vegetable garden, and the native persimmon and serviceberry tress scattered around campus. It dawned on us both that we could and should continue our poem correspondence with more of a direction and focus on the good work we were doing in our own backyards, work that very often leads to a line or more of poetry while we each work and fuss and fume over our plots of earth. In my former home in western New York, I focused much more on flower gardening—when those bulb catalogues full of perennials and shade-garden delights start arriving in the thick of winter here, I start dog-earring the pages of my new cravings, start sketching out where my new additions could go. Ross' own backyard is a marvel of sustenance for his kitchen and gifts for his friends. How lovely to be sent on my way back home with a few peppers and potatoes and a couple heads of garlic from his garden when my time with Ross and his students was over. Here, then, is how we made sense and record of a full year in our respective gardens. Over the course of the year, Ross was also able to visit my family and flower gardens before we boarded a train together for the Millay Artist's Colony in the Berkshires in upstate New York. There, we revised and finished this series of epistolary poems.

It is our hope that some of the pleasure and anxiety of tending these gardens—which is to say, tending to ourselves, our relationships, our earth—comes through in these poems, written over the course of about a year. There's bounty, yes; but there's loss and sorrow too: like a garden, like a life. But as the leaf buds start swelling, as they start, even, unfurling—right around the corner!—it's time to focus on bounty: sing at the crocuses, get those peas in. Make friends with someone who has a rhubarb patch. See if the community garden has a plot with your name on it.

—*A.N. & R.G*

SUMMER

I still marvel at all the people who first mapped the summer sky—
the pretty patterns from chalk and string they first pulled
across the fresh-swept floor. Every monster wishes their teeth
gleams louder than Vega, summer's brightest star. Every night
has its own delights: waxwing, paper moth, firefly larvae.
I would drink the red and blue stars if I thought my thin throat
could handle it. Even at the darkest hour, my garden throws
furtive dots of pale light to guide my steps: the bubble of fresh
egg-froth on a frog's back, the secret bloom of moonflowers
when the children have been tucked into their tiny beds.

O teaselburr and grasshopper— how you catch in the hem of my skirt
like a summer cough. It's exhausting, this desire. But I would never
trade it for any shiny marble. Would you? I love the silence
of sweat in these the slow days of summer. All the mysterious sounds
in the trees—like a sack of watches—while I tend to tomato plants
who have only thought to give four fruits this entire month.

—*A.N.*

It's true. No golden marble or treasure chest or even
tongue mapping me ankle to the cove behind my ear
quells that guttural tug by which I unwind bindweed
from each thorny raspberry cane, or clip the fish pepper
from its scaffolding, or swing my axe if need be.
With which I hack back the jackass branch
or beg the rampant sunchokes this way, or that.
Or dream beneath the currant's
myriad golden mouths.

Some days I catch glimpse of the hurdy-gurdy path I make
through this garden: ooh! the gooseberries aglow,
ooh! the lemon balm tufting up, ooh! wasps swilling the golden florets
of bolted kale, and Good Lord the strawberry flowers
are the pursed lips of ghosts
I want to know. Yes, today I am on my belly
for that scant perfume, this invisible parade
of dying and bloom.

—R.G.

AUTUMN

At the onset of fall, there are days full of the need
to exhale without sound around the crispy aquilegia
stalks. One last plume of astilbe is the only shot of pink left,
and even now drifts of unraked leaves threaten to choke
it out. I wouldn't wish this sickness on anyone.

The only sound I remember from that week
with you at summer's end was the terrible toss
of bullfrogs flinging themselves into the pond
when we approached. Wait. The only sound
I remember is actually a color, muddy river water

that hides an ancient fish. I never sat up nights
with sick horses and I wonder if that's
the difference: their coughs will never haunt me.
They say frogs are vanishing all over the Midwest,
but I can still hear them.

—*A.N.*

And yet, and yet, when the cold
makes brittle what remains—the spent okra
stalk, the few pepper plants that hung on
through the first two frosts, those little gold
tomatoes—when it withers even the rogue
amaranth, its tousled
mane bent and defeated,
when the silver maple out front has ceased whispering,
and when the bullfrogs nestle into their muddy lairs,
and the peepers go where they go,
and the crows circle,
just down the street, its leaves
too mostly blown off, spindly
and creaking in the wind,
while the whole world shimmers with death,
hauling all its sugar into perfect globes
the size of a child's handful,
giddy, it seems,
at the sound of ants
slurping beneath, at me
joining them, brushing away wood chip and beetle
before burying my tongue
in the burst pulp
dropped on the earth below,
the persimmon
gives its modest fruit
for yet a while.

—R.G.

                        Each fruit is a singular memory
    of earth-fire and juicy spit
    of summer days spent in tuck, in trim,
    in bend—twisting vines around a trellis
while a cardinal quilts a metallic chip
through the air.

    Now, only red prickleberries
of kousa dogwood pierce the grey landscape
when days are so dark all the solar lamps flicker
on at half-past three.

    I enter the season of naps, of the eye
I always kept open when my garden was
raked and cut like hibiscus' droopy mouths,
the woody stems of hydrangea and I cannot remember
when I last knelt on all fours.

    This warmest November in memory, this nicking
of little holes in the lawn to slip pearly bulbs of crocus
to naturalize—

    when I am too full, even the business
    of flies knocking at my globe light
    cannot capture your wild hum.

—*A.N.*

WINTER

And yesterday,
looking from my chilly kitchen
over the garden ice-slicked and shining:
crumpled tufts of asparagus fronds
slumbering beneath the cherry tree;
the knuckled grape vine gripping
its rickety fence like a fighter
between rounds. Strange,

then, when the full summer bloom—
not just half-waft, whiff or hint—
but the giddy lilac gust, honeysuckle gale,
gaudy burst whole of rugosa rose
sticker-thick and grabby;
the drag and flash of the apple's giddy show,
crinoline or crepe (words the meaning of which
I don't even know!), blowsing like a dancer's skirt;
when ruckus and sweet and plain good like this
my dead friend came to me,
some fragrant winter flower now,
his blend of incense and body
and wool overcoat frayed at the sleeves,
while a glaze of ice made all the bones of my garden shine.

—*R.G.*

This time I left. I could not swallow

these dark weeks of the new year
even though this is supposed to be
my season— the constellation of a goat
draped over us now is supposed
to comfort and stay the coils around
my heart. I thought I would regret I didn't plant
a line of skunk cabbage—so warm their flowers
can thaw fly wing and even melt snow—
but it turns out I never needed them.
When I returned from Florida:

no snow to inch over the barely-used woodpile,

no snow to reveal the mysterious visitors arriving at night,

no snow like pale kites cut and lost in a terrible wind,

no snow starfishing from the sky and onto a bleak beach,

no snow collected on the weak scatter of straw in the old berry patch

and the ground softens under my boot because
too many grosbeaks herald the sunrise and where
are these newly designed nests they've never had to build
like this: a lighter, brightly lit story of architecture and twig?

—*A.N.*

And maybe there's some other story:
the finger's plow furrowing a scar
for seeds through the loam,
and the way the flesh's million filaments
fleck like mica the soil
until it glows—no, no.
The earth is heating up, I mean to say.
Nothing like peach blossoms in February to tell you
something's off—when these
shivered and shimmied in the wind,
it was a full month early.
Do you know what I'm asking?
The garden these days leans in as if to say,
"You're fucked, friend."
It says so with equanimity, all its leaves
quaking through the bright light
like applause for the dead.
If the garden had shoulders, I think,
it'd shrug. Berries today,
the blue-jay dive-bombing the cat today,
the silver maple loosing its twirling battalions today,
desert tomorrow.
What am I trying to say?
The tiny prints of your kids' feet in the garden
filling with shadow?

—R.G.

SPRING

No shadows here, only mud.
Praise the caked up trowel, hand rake,
and grass scissor. I want to kiss each crumble
of sunbaked earth as my sons welcome iris
and drunk ants whirl-rush over each juicy peony bud.
After warm rains come the spring peepers shivering
out of the mud and sitting half in, half out of a puddle.
You must know the bees have come early
this year too: I see them visit aster, sweet Williams,
bleeding hearts, and azalea blossoms hardy enough
to not have crisped with the last late frost. Whatever light
bees give off after the last snow, I hold up to you now.

      I cannot explain the click-step of beetles.
You are on your own for that. I grew up with patience
for soil and stars. Lace & pyrite. I believe
in an underworld littered with gems.
In another life, I have to. Sometimes I lose track
of all the bees and their singing.

      You thought I said *stinging*.

—*A.N.*

Maybe you're right: let us stop explaining.
I saw those ants too—soon
they'll slurp caves into the handful of apples
that come on the pipsqueak tree out back,
or scurry dizzy on the sugar
glazing the sweetest bean I've ever tasted,
the beans themselves tonguing
through the spent cherry bush.
Terrified as I am—and I am—
the bumblebees furrow the pursed
and purple lips of false indigo
for the dusty blush
and I want to go make a hallelujah
of my own simple body. Not to mention
the cup plants just coming up out back
can hold mouthfuls of wet
despite the months-long drought.
All is never lost.
Some of what remains
of my father swims amidst the breathing
roots of the plum tree. You could almost
see him look out from the leaves' stomata
in spring, or his fingerprints pressed into
the delicate whorls of the young bark.
And when the tree makes its first
fruit next year, or the next,
it won't only be in dreams
he's back. I think I too will be
so lucky some day. Some day,
I think, so too will you be.

—*R.G.*

SUMMER

The plump & pink language of coneflowers is not found
in any dictionary—no translations available—not even
from a country with no apples. & now you've left me
trying to recreate a kiss of questions & fruit peel & grain

under the arches of snowball hydrangea. Even in this
drought, I go back to the garden so often because
I don't know yet how to function in a world without
my mother. I learn from her how to make it teem with life

even when lack of a decent rain seems to nudge us towards
a hundred thousand little deaths (if you count each crispy blade
& beetle shell). After a fox or squirrel visit, I sometimes find
a ruined blue eggshell under a robin nest, but the yard

never lacks their happy song: *Cheer up! Cheerily! Cheer up!*
You say all is never lost but how exactly do robins know
what first new branch to land on without a guide?
How did *you*? How do they learn to snip twig & bits

of cloth to pad their own nests? Someday I want to return
to the place where you've scattered hay underfoot,
the place where—when you least expect her—
a marbled cat comes singing of an invisible & delicious

thirst. & one day it will become clear you've smelled
the sickly sweet song of colrain bee balm before. You'll
remember the invisible lemon in your palm
& you'll remember this sad, soft question.

—*A.N.*

Above me, around me, swirls the constellation
of bees chasing fall's last flush:
the crook-necked aster
bent over near the brushpile; the sunchokes
plowing through it; goldenrod and some tiny grin of a plant
whose name I do not know purse their frilled mouths.
On the lip of the hive,
and in the scrub beneath, it looks like more lust,
pairs of bees snugged cheek to cheek. They twirl and flip
while above them, it looks like to me,
the day to day goes on. Usually one of them
flying away, and the other still or moored on one side,
maybe clutching upside down a stem of clover.
I put my finger down to one of the broken
trapped in a thicket of grass, and she reaches her tiny legs, touching a few times
before crawling up to the back of my hand. Her wings
shredded to lace. Stammering like an engine
not turning over. I hold her very close to my face.
The galaxy turning all around us.
Turning us all around.

—R.G.

Our Wholeness, Our Togetherness: A Conversation with Aimee Nezhukumatathil & Ross Gay

Ross Gay: What did collaboration make possible in your poetry for this project?

Aimee Nezhukumatathil: That's easy. As a writer with Type-A leanings, I learned how to give up control in my own writing process—control in drafts of poems and control in the finished poem. Of course, I mean that when I feel my writing is going well, it's precisely because I have "let go" a bit to chase down a metaphor or image, but there was always a steadiness to my writing. I've written poems for over twenty years now and that's no small feat to let my sense of control go in a collaboration. And yet, I was relieved—at least in our collaboration—because it very much felt like play and whimsy. Still, because they were epistolary with a writer whom I consider a friend and also one of my favorite poets alive, it was, I confess, scarier than I had anticipated. Our collaboration encouraged a vulnerability in me—for example, I believe it was the first time I ever broached the subject of ever losing my mother in a poem. Ever. How about you?

RG: Part of what I love about collaboration—and this kind of collaboration in particular, where you are automatically submitting to the process—means giving over to the sharing. Like: this thing is ours. That can be challenging, to be sure, because part of my inclination, a pretty big one, I have to say, is also controlling a thing, in this case, a poem. But there is this beautiful meeting of control and out-of-control that I think beautiful poems often come from, this interaction with mystery or something. You know, listening to something you don't quite know what and moving with it. I feel like collaborating, or collaborating well (and happily!) requires some of that. So, I think it made and makes me more able to listen generally.

AN: In which ways did our collaboration influence or push your own solo writing?

RG: Well there are poems that I would not have known how to write, or that I would not have known to write in the first place, had it not been for this collaboration. The poem "Burial" in *Catalogue* is a version, I think an expanded version of a poem that first arrived in our collaboration. And that arrived because of something you did, some direction you sent our little craft in. You were the wind that made that poem happen! I'm glad for that. Of course, the pleasure of the collaboration was also about trying to match, or interact beautifully with your intense and wonderful interaction with your garden. So what that kind of means is that I was inclined to look more closely at my own garden, to be more fully in my own garden, on account of the beautiful ways you were writing being in your garden. And that means, as if you didn't know, being happier.

AN: One of my favorite things about many of your poems is the sense of intimacy that is created by your line, your diction, and the long swoops of breathless sentences. When I teach your work, I know many of my students say that in reading your poems, they feel like a friend is talking to them. Anyone who knows the both of us personally knows that we can both be... let's say, effusive, when we are talking about something we love, be it a narwhal or a paw-paw fruit. So it is probably no surprise that when I was working on poems in my collection, Oceanic, I think there are a few poems where I found my sentences unspool a little longer than usual, especially when I was writing about wonderment. And that is a direct result of having you as one of my first readers—at that point, I was used to imagining you smile as you read say, one of my previous and extra effusive garden reports.

RG: How do you negotiate joy?

AN: Growing up in the 1970s and 80s, I didn't have many models or representations of Asian Americans expressing something as simple as happiness. What little representation there was involved violent assassins or caricatures like Long Duk Dong from *Sixteen Candles*. It's a heck of a thing to grow up without seeing anyone who looked like you even smile in a movie, music video, or TV show. It certainly didn't appear in any of the books I was taught or found in my libraries (and I was a voracious reader who was searching for it!). I think of that anytime I get nervous or worried that expressing joy or wonder in a poem might not be so-called "poem material," I think of that when I'm asked for a "serious" (i.e. non-smiling) author photo and I refuse, I think of that anytime I crack a goofy joke at a reading. Also, I'm a mom to two young sons and I'm so grateful that the media they consume now contains so much more diversity than the media I consumed as a kid. There's still a long way to go, but most of all I'm grateful that they get to have books and pop culture where it isn't so strange to see someone that looks like their mom expressing joy. And though I risk something by admitting that I love being their mom, that it truly brings me such happiness, I'm very conscious of them reading these poems down the line (my oldest sometimes reads them now, actually). But most importantly, I want them to always be able to know in deeds, not just in writing: We gave our mother so much joy. And finally, in writing about joy, I'm making a deliberate attempt to imagine and re-imagine the world.

RG: I am spending more and more time studying joy, in part because I suspect it is connected to (or one of the expressions of deep awareness of) love. And in part, too, because I think we have an obligation, like an ethical obligation, to study what we love, what we want to preserve and keep with us and grow. Joy strikes me as one of the ways we know we are in the midst of such things. It's like a finger pointing to the thing, saying "Take care of this!" Saying, "Sing about this!" That might be a gathering of beloveds or it might mean someone giving you directions, both of you using languages you do not speak fluently. It might mean the green birds in Barcelona, or the sound of kids' voices from somewhere you are not sure of. It might mean the creek like a xylophone when all the frogs hop in. Joy strikes me (it is funny that I am inclined to say that joy strikes me; this is a good strickenness, trust me) as, like, I don't quite know how to say it, because I was going to say a kind of fabric between us, but it's more like the way the fabric itself holds together. Joy alerts us to the moments when our alienation diminishes, or, even, disappears. It reminds us of our wholeness, our togetherness—which is the truth.

–Originally published in THE MARGINS, *from the Asian American Writers' Workshop (aaww.org)*

Acknowledgements

Selections from Lace & Pyrite originally appeared in the Jan/Feb 2014 issue of *Orion* magazine. Special thanks to former poetry editor Hannah Fries for her heroic support and encouragement for our collaboration.

Thanks to the Millay Colony for the time and the beautiful space to finish edits on these poems.

Thank you to the original publishers of this collaboration at Organic Weapon Arts Publishing.

Printed in the USA
CPSIA information can be obtained
at www.ICGtesting.com
LVHW090735130524
780071LV00005B/395